My Martial Arts Lessons

A journal of my skills,
my progress, and
my achievements.

Karleen Tauszik

TIP
TOP
BOOKS

Published by Tip Top Books, Dunedin, Florida

Text and layout copyright © 2021 by Karleen Tauszik
Cover Illustration from BigstockPhoto.com, photo 411837172, contributor kozyrevaelena.
Cover Design Copyright © 2021 by Karleen Tauszik
Cover design and cover photo editing by Karleen Tauszik

Summary: This journal provides children with a place to track their martial arts lessons and monitor their practices, their areas of improvement, their goals, and their fun memories.

ISBN-13: 978-1-954130-20-3

Karleen Tauszik is the author of books for children ages 8-12. Visit her on the web at KarleenT.com, where you can see her other books and sign up for her newsletter.

This book belongs to

_____

It records my martial arts lessons

from _____ to _____

              Date   Date

How to Use This Special Book

This journal is the perfect place to track your martial arts lessons—what you learn, how you progress, your achievements, the highlights, and all the fun you have.

Here's what you'll find inside:

First, there's a sheet where you can fill in where you're at in your martial arts skills and where you hope to be when you finish your lessons.

After that, it's time to get started! There are enough pages to journal up to 50 lessons, so you have enough for a full year if you use one each week. There's also an extra page reserved for photocopying in case you need it.

Every time you complete ten lesson pages, you'll find a "Looking Back" page, where you can assess your progress from the previous ten weeks.

At the end, there are five blank pages to fill with photos, extra notes, and mementos. You can even get your friends from your lessons to write notes and their autographs. Add whatever you want to so you remember your martial arts lessons and make this book uniquely yours.

Getting Started

As you start your lessons, rate your level of martial arts skills by circling the number that applies:

1	2	3	4	5	6	7	8	9	10
Beginner				Intermediate					Award-winning

At what level would you like to be by the time you finish this journal? Why?

_____

_____

_____

What do think will be your greatest challenge? _____

_____

_____

_____

How do you feel about starting your lessons? _____

_____

_____

_____

What's the first thing you'd like to accomplish? _____

_____

_____

_____

Use this extra space to write any other thoughts or goals you have before you start your lessons.

MY LESSON on _____
Day & Date

Things I learned in this lesson are: _____

_____

_____

_____

Feedback from my instructor was: _____

_____

_____

_____

Things I think I did well are: _____

_____

_____

_____

Things I could have done better are: _____

_____

_____

_____

Before my next lesson, I can work on improving by: _____

_____

_____

_____

MY LESSON on _____

Day & Date

Things I learned in this lesson are: _____

_____

_____

_____

Feedback from my instructor was: _____

_____

_____

_____

Things I think I did well are: _____

_____

_____

_____

Things I could have done better are: _____

_____

_____

_____

Before my next lesson, I can work on improving by: _____

_____

_____

_____

MY LESSON on _____

Things I learned in this lesson are: _____

_____

_____

_____

Feedback from my instructor was: _____

_____

_____

_____

Things I think I did well are: _____

_____

_____

_____

Things I could have done better are: _____

_____

_____

_____

Before my next lesson, I can work on improving by: _____

_____

_____

_____

MY LESSON on _____

Day & Date

Things I learned in this lesson are: _____

_____

_____

_____

Feedback from my instructor was: _____

_____

_____

_____

Things I think I did well are: _____

_____

_____

_____

Things I could have done better are: _____

_____

_____

_____

Before my next lesson, I can work on improving by: _____

_____

_____

_____

MY LESSON on _____

Day & Date

Things I learned in this lesson are: _____

_____

_____

_____

Feedback from my instructor was: _____

_____

_____

_____

Things I think I did well are: _____

_____

_____

_____

Things I could have done better are: _____

_____

_____

_____

Before my next lesson, I can work on improving by: _____

_____

_____

_____

MY LESSON on _____

Day & Date

Things I learned in this lesson are: _____

_____

_____

_____

Feedback from my instructor was: _____

_____

_____

_____

Things I think I did well are: _____

_____

_____

_____

Things I could have done better are: _____

_____

_____

_____

Before my next lesson, I can work on improving by: _____

_____

_____

_____

MY LESSON on

Day & Date

Things I learned in this lesson are:

_____

_____

_____

Feedback from my instructor was:

_____

_____

_____

Things I think I did well are:

_____

_____

_____

Things I could have done better are:

_____

_____

_____

Before my next lesson, I can work on improving by:

_____

_____

_____

MY LESSON on _____
Day & Date

Things I learned in this lesson are: _____

_____

_____

_____

Feedback from my instructor was: _____

_____

_____

_____

Things I think I did well are: _____

_____

_____

_____

Things I could have done better are: _____

_____

_____

_____

Before my next lesson, I can work on improving by: _____

_____

_____

MY LESSON on _____

Day & Date

Things I learned in this lesson are: _____

_____

_____

_____

Feedback from my instructor was: _____

_____

_____

_____

Things I think I did well are: _____

_____

_____

_____

Things I could have done better are: _____

_____

_____

_____

Before my next lesson, I can work on improving by: _____

_____

_____

_____

MY LESSON on

Day & Date

Things I learned in this lesson are:

Feedback from my instructor was:

Things I think I did well are:

Things I could have done better are:

Before my next lesson, I can work on improving by:

LOOKING BACK over the past ten lessons…

In what areas have you improved since your first lesson?

_____

_____

_____

_____

What has been your greatest challenge and how did you overcome it?

_____

_____

_____

_____

What has been your greatest accomplishment?

_____

_____

_____

_____

What are you looking forward to learning next?

_____

_____

_____

_____

MY LESSON on _____

Things I learned in this lesson are: _____

_____

_____

_____

Feedback from my instructor was: _____

_____

_____

_____

Things I think I did well are: _____

_____

_____

_____

Things I could have done better are: _____

_____

_____

_____

Before my next lesson, I can work on improving by: _____

_____

_____

_____

MY LESSON on _____

Day & Date

Things I learned in this lesson are: _____

_____

_____

_____

Feedback from my instructor was: _____

_____

_____

_____

Things I think I did well are: _____

_____

_____

_____

Things I could have done better are: _____

_____

_____

_____

Before my next lesson, I can work on improving by: _____

_____

_____

_____

MY LESSON on _____
Day & Date

Things I learned in this lesson are: _____

_____

_____

_____

Feedback from my instructor was: _____

_____

_____

Things I think I did well are: _____

_____

_____

Things I could have done better are: _____

_____

_____

Before my next lesson, I can work on improving by: _____

_____

_____

_____

MY LESSON on

Things I learned in this lesson are: _____

_____

_____

_____

Feedback from my instructor was: _____

_____

_____

_____

Things I think I did well are: _____

_____

_____

_____

Things I could have done better are: _____

_____

_____

_____

Before my next lesson, I can work on improving by: _____

_____

_____

_____

MY LESSON on _____

Things I learned in this lesson are: _____

_____

_____

_____

Feedback from my instructor was: _____

_____

_____

_____

Things I think I did well are: _____

_____

_____

_____

Things I could have done better are: _____

_____

_____

_____

Before my next lesson, I can work on improving by: _____

_____

_____

_____

MY LESSON on _____

Things I learned in this lesson are: _____

_____

_____

_____

Feedback from my instructor was: _____

_____

_____

_____

Things I think I did well are: _____

_____

_____

_____

Things I could have done better are: _____

_____

_____

_____

Before my next lesson, I can work on improving by: _____

_____

_____

_____

MY LESSON on _____

Things I learned in this lesson are: _____

_____

_____

_____

Feedback from my instructor was: _____

_____

_____

_____

Things I think I did well are: _____

_____

_____

_____

Things I could have done better are: _____

_____

_____

_____

Before my next lesson, I can work on improving by: _____

_____

_____

_____

MY LESSON on _____

Things I learned in this lesson are: _____

_____

_____

_____

Feedback from my instructor was: _____

_____

_____

_____

Things I think I did well are: _____

_____

_____

_____

Things I could have done better are: _____

_____

_____

_____

Before my next lesson, I can work on improving by: _____

_____

_____

_____

MY LESSON on _____
Day & Date

Things I learned in this lesson are: _____

_____

_____

_____

Feedback from my instructor was: _____

_____

_____

_____

Things I think I did well are: _____

_____

_____

_____

Things I could have done better are: _____

_____

_____

_____

Before my next lesson, I can work on improving by: _____

_____

_____

_____

MY LESSON on _____
Day & Date

Things I learned in this lesson are: _____

_____

_____

_____

Feedback from my instructor was: _____

_____

_____

_____

Things I think I did well are: _____

_____

_____

_____

Things I could have done better are: _____

_____

_____

_____

Before my next lesson, I can work on improving by: _____

_____

_____

_____

LOOKING BACK over the past ten lessons…

In what areas have you improved since you started these ten lessons?

_____

_____

_____

_____

What has been your greatest challenge and how did you overcome it?

_____

_____

_____

_____

What has been your greatest accomplishment?

_____

_____

_____

_____

What are you looking forward to learning next?

_____

_____

_____

_____

MY LESSON on _____

Things I learned in this lesson are: _____

_____

_____

_____

Feedback from my instructor was: _____

_____

_____

_____

Things I think I did well are: _____

_____

_____

_____

Things I could have done better are: _____

_____

_____

_____

Before my next lesson, I can work on improving by: _____

_____

_____

_____

MY LESSON on _____

Things I learned in this lesson are: _____

_____

_____

_____

Feedback from my instructor was: _____

_____

_____

_____

Things I think I did well are: _____

_____

_____

_____

Things I could have done better are: _____

_____

_____

_____

Before my next lesson, I can work on improving by: _____

_____

_____

_____

MY LESSON on

Day & Date

Things I learned in this lesson are:

_____

_____

_____

_____

Feedback from my instructor was:

_____

_____

_____

Things I think I did well are:

_____

_____

_____

Things I could have done better are:

_____

_____

_____

Before my next lesson, I can work on improving by:

_____

_____

_____

MY LESSON on _____

Day & Date

Things I learned in this lesson are: _____

_____

_____

_____

Feedback from my instructor was: _____

_____

_____

_____

Things I think I did well are: _____

_____

_____

_____

Things I could have done better are: _____

_____

_____

_____

Before my next lesson, I can work on improving by: _____

_____

_____

_____

MY LESSON on

Things I learned in this lesson are:

Feedback from my instructor was:

Things I think I did well are:

Things I could have done better are:

Before my next lesson, I can work on improving by:

MY LESSON on _____

Things I learned in this lesson are: _____

_____

_____

_____

Feedback from my instructor was: _____

_____

_____

_____

Things I think I did well are: _____

_____

_____

_____

Things I could have done better are: _____

_____

_____

_____

Before my next lesson, I can work on improving by: _____

_____

_____

_____

MY LESSON on

Things I learned in this lesson are:

_____

_____

_____

Feedback from my instructor was:

_____

_____

_____

Things I think I did well are:

_____

_____

_____

Things I could have done better are:

_____

_____

_____

Before my next lesson, I can work on improving by:

_____

_____

_____

MY LESSON on _____

Day & Date

Things I learned in this lesson are: _____

_____

_____

_____

Feedback from my instructor was: _____

_____

_____

_____

Things I think I did well are: _____

_____

_____

_____

Things I could have done better are: _____

_____

_____

_____

Before my next lesson, I can work on improving by: _____

_____

_____

MY LESSON on _____

Things I learned in this lesson are: _____

_____

_____

_____

Feedback from my instructor was: _____

_____

_____

_____

Things I think I did well are: _____

_____

_____

_____

Things I could have done better are: _____

_____

_____

_____

Before my next lesson, I can work on improving by: _____

_____

_____

_____

MY LESSON on _____

Things I learned in this lesson are: _____

_____

_____

_____

Feedback from my instructor was: _____

_____

_____

_____

Things I think I did well are: _____

_____

_____

_____

Things I could have done better are: _____

_____

_____

_____

Before my next lesson, I can work on improving by: _____

_____

_____

_____

LOOKING BACK over the past ten lessons…

In what areas have you improved since you started these ten lessons?

What has been your greatest challenge and how did you overcome it?

What has been your greatest accomplishment?

What are you looking forward to learning next?

MY LESSON on _____

Things I learned in this lesson are: _____

_____

_____

_____

Feedback from my instructor was: _____

_____

_____

_____

Things I think I did well are: _____

_____

_____

_____

Things I could have done better are: _____

_____

_____

_____

Before my next lesson, I can work on improving by: _____

_____

_____

_____

MY LESSON on

<u>Day & Date</u>

Things I learned in this lesson are: _____

_____

_____

_____

Feedback from my instructor was: _____

_____

_____

_____

Things I think I did well are: _____

_____

_____

_____

Things I could have done better are: _____

_____

_____

_____

Before my next lesson, I can work on improving by: _____

_____

_____

_____

MY LESSON on _____

Day & Date

Things I learned in this lesson are: _____

_____

_____

_____

Feedback from my instructor was: _____

_____

_____

_____

Things I think I did well are: _____

_____

_____

_____

Things I could have done better are: _____

_____

_____

_____

Before my next lesson, I can work on improving by: _____

_____

_____

_____

MY LESSON on

_____
Day & Date

Things I learned in this lesson are: _____

_____

_____

_____

Feedback from my instructor was: _____

_____

_____

_____

Things I think I did well are: _____

_____

_____

_____

Things I could have done better are: _____

_____

_____

_____

Before my next lesson, I can work on improving by: _____

_____

_____

_____

MY LESSON on ....

Day & Date

Things I learned in this lesson are: ....

....

....

....

Feedback from my instructor was: ....

....

....

....

Things I think I did well are: ....

....

....

....

Things I could have done better are: ....

....

....

....

Before my next lesson, I can work on improving by: ....

....

....

....

MY LESSON on _____

Things I learned in this lesson are: _____

_____

_____

_____

Feedback from my instructor was: _____

_____

_____

_____

Things I think I did well are: _____

_____

_____

_____

Things I could have done better are: _____

_____

_____

_____

Before my next lesson, I can work on improving by: _____

_____

_____

_____

MY LESSON on _____

Things I learned in this lesson are: _____

_____

_____

_____

Feedback from my instructor was: _____

_____

_____

_____

Things I think I did well are: _____

_____

_____

_____

Things I could have done better are: _____

_____

_____

_____

Before my next lesson, I can work on improving by: _____

_____

_____

_____

MY LESSON on

Day & Date

Things I learned in this lesson are:

_____

_____

_____

Feedback from my instructor was:

_____

_____

_____

Things I think I did well are:

_____

_____

_____

Things I could have done better are:

_____

_____

_____

Before my next lesson, I can work on improving by:

_____

_____

_____

MY LESSON on

Things I learned in this lesson are:

Feedback from my instructor was:

Things I think I did well are:

Things I could have done better are:

Before my next lesson, I can work on improving by:

MY LESSON on _____

Day & Date

Things I learned in this lesson are: _____

_____

_____

_____

Feedback from my instructor was: _____

_____

_____

_____

Things I think I did well are: _____

_____

_____

_____

Things I could have done better are: _____

_____

_____

_____

Before my next lesson, I can work on improving by: _____

_____

_____

_____

LOOKING BACK over the past ten lessons...

In what areas have you improved since you started these ten lessons?

_____

_____

_____

_____

What has been your greatest challenge and how did you overcome it?

_____

_____

_____

_____

What has been your greatest accomplishment?

_____

_____

_____

_____

What are you looking forward to learning next?

_____

_____

_____

_____

MY LESSON on _____

Things I learned in this lesson are: _____

_____

_____

_____

Feedback from my instructor was: _____

_____

_____

_____

Things I think I did well are: _____

_____

_____

_____

Things I could have done better are: _____

_____

_____

_____

Before my next lesson, I can work on improving by: _____

_____

_____

_____

MY LESSON on

Things I learned in this lesson are: _____

_____

_____

_____

Feedback from my instructor was: _____

_____

_____

_____

Things I think I did well are: _____

_____

_____

_____

Things I could have done better are: _____

_____

_____

_____

Before my next lesson, I can work on improving by: _____

_____

_____

_____

MY LESSON on _____

Things I learned in this lesson are: _____

_____

_____

_____

Feedback from my instructor was: _____

_____

_____

_____

Things I think I did well are: _____

_____

_____

_____

Things I could have done better are: _____

_____

_____

_____

Before my next lesson, I can work on improving by: _____

_____

_____

_____

MY LESSON on

Day & Date

Things I learned in this lesson are:

Feedback from my instructor was:

Things I think I did well are:

Things I could have done better are:

Before my next lesson, I can work on improving by:

MY LESSON on _____

Day & Date

Things I learned in this lesson are: _____

_____

_____

_____

Feedback from my instructor was: _____

_____

_____

_____

Things I think I did well are: _____

_____

_____

_____

Things I could have done better are: _____

_____

_____

_____

Before my next lesson, I can work on improving by: _____

_____

_____

_____

MY LESSON on _____

Day & Date

Things I learned in this lesson are: _____

_____

_____

_____

Feedback from my instructor was: _____

_____

_____

_____

Things I think I did well are: _____

_____

_____

_____

Things I could have done better are: _____

_____

_____

_____

Before my next lesson, I can work on improving by: _____

_____

_____

MY LESSON on _____

Things I learned in this lesson are: _____

_____

_____

_____

Feedback from my instructor was: _____

_____

_____

_____

Things I think I did well are: _____

_____

_____

_____

Things I could have done better are: _____

_____

_____

_____

Before my next lesson, I can work on improving by: _____

_____

_____

_____

MY LESSON on _____

Things I learned in this lesson are: _____

_____

_____

_____

Feedback from my instructor was: _____

_____

_____

_____

Things I think I did well are: _____

_____

_____

_____

Things I could have done better are: _____

_____

_____

_____

Before my next lesson, I can work on improving by: _____

_____

_____

_____

MY LESSON on _____

Things I learned in this lesson are: _____

_____

_____

_____

Feedback from my instructor was: _____

_____

_____

_____

Things I think I did well are: _____

_____

_____

_____

Things I could have done better are: _____

_____

_____

_____

Before my next lesson, I can work on improving by: _____

_____

_____

_____

MY LESSON on _____

Things I learned in this lesson are: _____

_____

_____

_____

Feedback from my instructor was: _____

_____

_____

_____

Things I think I did well are: _____

_____

_____

_____

Things I could have done better are: _____

_____

_____

_____

Before my next lesson, I can work on improving by: _____

_____

_____

_____

LOOKING BACK over the past ten lessons…

In what areas have you improved since you started these last ten lessons?

_____

_____

_____

_____

What has been your greatest challenge and how did you overcome it?

_____

_____

_____

_____

What has been your greatest accomplishment?

_____

_____

_____

_____

Now look back at the Getting Started page to see how much you've learned and improved through these lessons. What have been the biggest changes in your skills?

_____

_____

_____

If you've used up all 50 of your

worksheet sets,

there's one more after this page.

Use it to make as many

photocopies as you need

to complete your lessons.

MY LESSON on _____

Day & Date

Things I learned in this lesson are: _____

_____

_____

_____

Feedback from my instructor was: _____

_____

_____

_____

Things I think I did well are: _____

_____

_____

_____

Things I could have done better are: _____

_____

_____

_____

Before my next lesson, I can work on improving by: _____

_____

_____

_____

My
Martial Arts
Lesson
Memories

About the Author

Karleen Tauszik writes books mostly for children ages 8 to 12. Her goal as an author is to get kids to LOVE reading. She is married to a professional ventriloquist and magician, and they live in the Tampa Bay area.

Other lesson journals by Karleen include:
>   My Gymnastics Lessons
>   My Dance Lessons
>   My Ballet Lessons
>   My Horseback Riding Lessons
>   My Swimming Lessons
>   My Archery Lessons
>   My Ice Skating Lessons

Karleen has also created a similar series for team sports:
>   My Baseball Season
>   My Softball Season
>   My Soccer Season
>   My Football Season
>   My Cheerleading Season
>   My Volleyball Season
>   My Hockey Season
>   My Basketball Season

Find links to all of these books and more at KarleenT.com.

Made in United States
North Haven, CT
01 July 2022

20831652R00043